Beautiful
Oklahoma

Oklahoma

State Capital: *Oklahoma City*
State Flower: *Mistletoe*
State Nickname: *Sooner State*
State Bird: *Scissor-tailed flycatcher*
State Animal: *Bison*
State Colors: *Green and white*

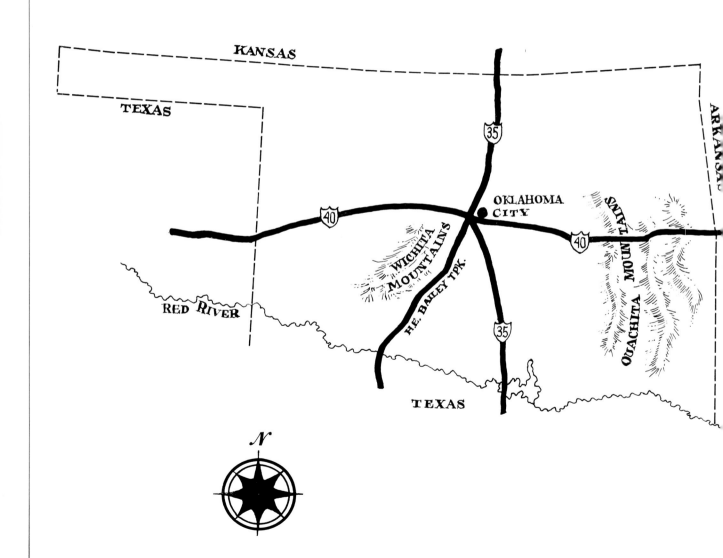

Beautiful
Oklahoma

Concept and Design: Robert D. Shangle
Text: Brian Berger

First Printing June, 1980
Published by Beautiful America Publishing Company
P.O. Box 608, Beaverton, Oregon 97075
Robert D. Shangle, Publisher

Library of Congress Cataloging in Publication Data
Beautiful Oklahoma
1. Oklahoma—Description and travel—1951—Views. I. Title.
F695.B47   1980   917.66'0022'2   80 10968
ISBN 0-89802-008-5
ISBN 0-89802-007-7 (paperback)

Photo Credits

jERRY SIEVE—*page 20; page 29; page 30; page 34; pages 36-37; page 38; page 40; page 42; page 47; page 49; page 50; page 52; page 53; page 54; page 55; page 58; page 61; page 63; page 64.*

BOB TAYLOR—*page 18; page 19; page 22; page 35; page 39; page 41; page 43; page 51.*

BRUCE and SAM WHITE—*page 17; page 21; page 23; pages 24-25; page 26; page 27; page 28; page 31; page 32; page 33; page 44; page 45; page 46; page 48; pages 56-57; page 59; page 60; page 62.*

Enlarged Prints

Most of the photography in this book is available as photographic enlargements. Send self-addressed, stamped envelope for information. For a complete product catalog, send $1.00.
Beautiful America Publishing Company
P.O. Box 608
Beaverton. Oregon 97075

Contents

Introduction

Oklahoma! To Rogers and Hammerstein it was: "Flowers on the prairie where the June bugs zoom/Plenty of air and plenty of room . . . ." To the Cherokee, Chickasaw, Choctaw, Creek, and Seminole Indians, this land provided the last hope of refuge from the expansionist policy of the land-grabbing white man to the east. To thousands of pioneer families looking for a fresh start in a new land, Oklahoma offered the chance for them to acquire 160 acres on lands previously ceded to the Indians—lands the Indians had been told would be theirs for "as long as grass shall grow and waters run."

Oklahoma! "Where the wind comes sweepin' down the plain" with strength enough to bend a crowbar, and where one might care to stay indoors if they see that same crowbar break. Oklahoma! Mother to gushers of oil, and the one-time "Oil Capital of the World." Oklahoma! A leader in crops and livestock, but still licking its wounds from the dust bowl years, when thousands of disillusioned farmers left the state and the bitter sight of their eroded farmlands.

In the language of the Choctaw, *Okla* means "people" and *homma* means "red," making Oklahoma the Land of the Red People. That's still true today; Oklahoma has nearly 100,000 full-blooded Indians, more than any state in the Union. If one were to count those that are one-half Indian, that figure might reach 200,000; and it would climb to a half-million if those who can claim only a trace of Native American blood in their veins were counted. Of the original 67 tribes that resided in Indian Territory during the early 1800s, 35 now make Oklahoma their home. Adapting as they have to the culture of the white man, they still cling to their colorful heritage, mixing the advanced technologies of a burgeoning industrial empire with the ornate ceremonial customs of a not-too-distant past.

The saga of the Oklahoma cowboy is also a colorful chapter in the state's short history of settlement. It is a chapter filled with stories of longhorn cattle drives and notorious desperados. Tall tales abound about the Oklahoma cowboy's expertise with a six-shooter and his ability to survive all hardships. One such tale recalls a marksmanship contest between two rival cowpokes: after shooting an equal number of barbs off a wire fence at a mile's distance, they reloaded their barrels with barbs and glue, and shot them *back* on the fence to see who was *really* good. Another story tells of the time a cowboy had a run-in with a group of outlaws. Deciding to get rid of the poor cowpoke the meanest way possible, the bandits stuffed him into a barrel and left him on the prairie to die. As luck would have it, along came an unsuspecting buffalo to investigate the situation. The critter just happened to drop his tail through an open knothole, where it was seized by the barrel's desperate occupant and only released when the bewildered and frightened beast had dragged him to the nearest town.

Oklahoma! Where the weather is forever the topic of conversation; and where, as Will Rogers said of it: "If you don't like it . . . wait a minute." Oklahoma! A land whose summers (in some places) can fry an egg, and whose winters can freeze a polar bear, but is mostly comfortable, with a mean annual temperature of 60.5 degrees.

Oklahoma! Its lakes and rivers provide a wealth of watersport activities while acting as sources of hydroelectric power and irrigation water. A huge source of such power comes from the McClellan-Kerr Arkansas River Navigation System (costing more to build than the Panama Canal and the St. Lawrence Seaway combined), a commercial waterway to the Gulf of Mexico. Before completion of this massive project, built to facilitate navigation and control flood waters, the state, at times, had more water than it liked. As Will Rogers once noted: "When the Arkansas, Red River, Salt Fork, Verdigris, Caney, Cat Creek, Possum Creek, Dog Creek, and Skunk Branch all are up after a rain, we got more seacoast than Australia."

Settled almost overnight by the onrush of thousands of impatient pioneers chafing at the bit to reach the most desirable homesteads in her "Unassigned Lands," Oklahoma's settlers quickly earned the name "Sooners," (those that found ways to enter the area before the official opening of the territory). This was a term later to become popular when referring to these alert, ambitious, and enterprising people of Oklahoma. Sooners today show these qualities in their burgeoning business and industrial markets, and in their outstanding achievements in the fields of music, drama, art, and architecture. It is also seen in their "people development through educational excellence" program, which results in a greater-than-average number of high school students who enter Oklahoma's colleges.

Since 1907, Sooners have rapidly changed the face of Oklahoma, carving from its sagebrush vistas and forested areas shining cities with modern high-rises, plazas, malls and fountains. One-quarter heavily forested, the state produces wood products that are valued at $50 million annually. An abundance of tall and short grasses fatten herds of cattle, an industry worth in excess of one billion dollars. Oil, still the state's most valued mineral resource, accounts for 94 percent of its mineral wealth. Rodeos and Indian ceremonials keep Oklahoma's heritage alive, allowing visitors a closeup look at the rich pageantry of a vanished era. Recreationally and historically, Oklahoma retains much of the romance of its pioneer past, affording the visitor the nearly unsullied landscape of a brand new state, and an early cultural atmosphere that will prompt those that would partake of it all to say: ''Yeeow! A-yip-i-o-ee-ay! Oklahoma, O.K.''

Brian Berger

Southeast

In the Southeast quadrant of Oklahoma, the drama of the Indians' struggle to retain their hunting lands against the weight of the white man's westward expansionist policy was played out. Forced to the lands west of the Mississippi (beginning in the fall of 1838) by land-hungry pioneers, the "Five Civilized Tribes"—Cherokee, Seminole, Choctaw, Creek, and Chickasaw—were herded by government soldiers from their homes in the old south, on the long, infamous march known as the "Trail of Tears." Perhaps 4,000 of an original 15,000 Indians perished before reaching the eastern border of what is now Oklahoma (then known as "Indian Territory"), victims of exhaustion, hunger, and white man's diseases. Here the Indians were to be offered a new beginning, safe from future government encroachments.

Arriving first in the new territory, the Choctaw settled in the southeastern portion. They were followed by the Chickasaw to the west of them, the Cherokee to the north, and the Creek and Seminole to their northwest. Quick to adapt to this new land, the Indians drew comfort from its physical beauties. It was beautiful country as was noted in the diary of a Swiss youth (Count de Pourtales) who traveled in company with Washington Irving through Oklahoma's eastern portions in 1832:

> "Nowhere have I ever seen so many deer, moose, bear, and turkey tracks ....We spent the morning in one of the most beautiful stretches of forest that I have ever seen .... [Here] were twenty varieties of climbing plants, some bright green and others delicately shaped and turned red by the frost .... The ground was covered with thick waves of horse-bean plants, forming an impenetrable, tangled carpet lifted up but not pierced by the underbrush."

Here the Indians adopted written constitutions, established school systems, and started a bilingual newspaper, *The Cherokee Advocate*. Many dressed in the clothes of the white man, and some were extremely enterprising, developing huge plantations that employed hundreds of slaves. Sixty years later, after numerous abuses of their treaty rights, Congress passed its final judgement on the lands of the Five Civilized Tribes: it authorized the "division of their properties, and the end of their government."

There is much to mourn in the dissolution of the Oklahoma Indians' unique society: theirs was a way of life that recognized the delicate balance that exists between man and his natural surroundings. Happily, Sooners have retained much of the Indians' respect for the environment and in doing so, have preserved most of the beauty of Oklahoma's natural environs. Their understanding has led to programs designed to conserve and, at times, enhance southeastern Oklahoma's rugged mountains, primal forests, and miles of clear-running streams. Man-made lakes have turned this into a popular fishing and hunting ground, and modern resorts line the sparkling lakefronts. In LeFlore County, the Ouachita Mountains form the most rugged topography of this region. Created by faulted layers of sandstone, the valleys of the Ouachitas follow narrow paths, channeling the chilly waters of reflective streams fed by hidden springs. A National Scenic Highway (State 1) follows the ridge of the Ouachitas for 60 memorable miles, offering an almost unobstructed view of this vast and variegated National Forest area.

Northwest of these thickly forested ridges lies giant Lake Eufaula. With nearly 600 miles of winding shoreline amid oak-covered hills, this reservoir, stocked with an abundance of black bass and catfish, is a favorite gathering spot for the area's fishermen. Places to camp and picnic are plentiful along its shores, two of the most noteworthy being Fountainhead and Arrowhead state parks. Both will treat the visitor to the forested greenery of thousands of acres laced with nature trails. They provide picnic tables, trailer spaces, shower facilities, boat rentals, horseback riding, swimming, and even an 18-hole golf course. Though generally exhibiting a placid nature, the lake's purplish-blue water can quickly show its cantankerous qualities when nudged by strong spring winds that agitate it into a rolling chop. More than anyone else, boaters should be aware of this change of mood, for it can happen in a matter of minutes.

The grave of Belle Starr is just east of Lake Eufaula, on a knoll overlooking the Canadian River. Packing two pistols strapped tightly around her slim waist, she rode with the likes of the James Brothers and could shoot with the best of them. Notorious as a horse thief and a bank robber, Starr quickly became known in real and fictionalized accounts as ''The Bandit Queen.'' As was the case with many of the outlaws of her day, Starr met her death at the business end of a shotgun (the killer was never caught) and was buried at Younger's Bend, near Lake Eufaula Dam. Recalling both her hard and gentle qualities, the epitaph marking her grave reads: ''Shed not for her the bitter tear/Nor give the heart to vain regret/Tis but the casket that lies here,/The gem that filled it sparkles yet.''

Oklahoma's miles of shoreline have been the result of its dam building efforts, which have transformed once-scarce water supplies into popular water-sport playgrounds. Southeastern Oklahoma has more than its share of these sparkling resort and recreation areas. Besides Lake Eufaula's 102,500 acres of water, there is the 680-mile shoreline of Lake Texoma. Located about 12 miles west of the city of Durant, Texoma is considered one of Oklahoma's leading playgrounds. Attracting an annual pilgrimage of over 11 million visitors with the excellence of its fishing, hunting, and watersport activities, the lake is also the home of the sumptuous Texoma Resort, operated by the state. Surrounding the lake are 24 public use areas and plenty of camping spots for those wishing to nestle into the greenery of the scenic shoreline. Close by, the Tishomingo National Wildlife Refuge (a 16,600-acre sportsman's paradise) on the Washita River is a favorite of waterfowl and deer hunters. Picnic and camping facilities, together with special viewing points for those who wish to observe the refuge's more than 200 bird species, offer solace from the weekday "battle."

Another favorite retreat, containing a smaller body of water (Arbuckle Reservoir), is the Chickasaw National Wildlife Refuge, some distance northwest of Lake Texoma. The refuge, containing 9,700 acres, has gained a reputation for its mineral waters. Numerous small waterfalls agitate clear-running streams as they wind their way through the refuge's wooded sections. A relic of Oklahoma's frontier past, a small buffalo herd is allowed to roam the Wildlife Refuge. They are descendants of the mighty hordes that fed on the lush grasses covering the state in an earlier time. Nature walks are a favorite summertime activity of visitors, and special programs are conducted for children.

Many cities dot this land of lakes, streams and mountains. Three of them, Shawnee, Ardmore, and McAlester, contain some of the largest populations. Shawnee began its growth as a trading post in 1872, witness to the great trail drives of Texas longhorns as they passed on their way south to Kansas. The railroads reached the town by 1895, bringing with them new businesses and more people. Oil from the Greater Seminole Oil Field boom caused the town's population to swell even further. Today Shawnee's economy remains healthy with a diversified industry, producers of such goods as electronic components, modular homes, work clothes, and processed foods. Visitors will want to take the opportunity to examine the town's historic structures (many of which are on the National Register of Historic Places), then perhaps enjoy a stroll in the greenery of the town's Woodland Park, offering "in-town" recreation. Ten miles northeast of town, near Prague, is the birthplace of

Jim Thorpe. Of Sac and Fox Indian blood, Thorpe was perhaps the greatest all-around athlete of his time. Entering the 1912 Olympics, he stunned the sports world by dominating its two most grueling events, the decathlon and pentathlon.

On the "sunny side" of the Arbuckle Mountains lies the city of Ardmore. The town has grown from a whistle stop on the tracks of the Santa Fe Railroad to one whose industries now generate an annual payroll of $25 million. Largest of these is the Uniroyal tire plant. Oil flowing from the Healdton field in 1913 gave the city its original stimulus for growth. Edging Ardmore's borders just south of the city, Lake Murray sits amid parklands, providing some 15,000 acres of recreational territory for residents and visitors alike. The lake's excellent resort hotel, with 54 rooms and 86 cabins, is a comfortable base from which to sample the area's golfing, tennis, sailboating, swimming and fishing.

McAlester, at the junction of U.S. Highway 69 and State 31, can be identified at night from miles around by the bright glow from a great copper sphere rising 170 feet from street level, crowning the beautiful architecture of its Rainbow Temple. Shining through 168 multi-colored lenses, the sphere's powerful beam is broken into jewel-like rays that area residents know best as the "light of Masonry." Coal was the principal ingredient responsible for McAlester's early growth. Later this was supplemented by the opening of Oklahoma State Penitentiary (Big Mac) and the establishment in 1942 of a Naval Ammunition Depot, which today employs 2,000 persons. A relic from the town's early coal-mining days, now housed at Frisco Depot, is a 5,000-pound chunk of the black mineral cut from a nearby tunnel in 1921. It is believed to be the largest ever mined.

The towns of Durant, Hugo and Isabel provide ideal stepping stones for visitors wishing to enjoy recreational opportunities afforded by lush forested areas and the coolness of lakes and streams. Durant is an important agricultural center and home of the beautiful campus of Southeastern Oklahoma State University. Hugo and Isabel are located in the heart of the lumber industry.

Northeast

Northeastern Oklahoma is a study of man's ability to mold his environment in ways that are beneficial, rather than just opportunistic. Once an area of marginal scrubland, the face of northeastern Oklahoma has been changed by ambitious dam building efforts. Thousands of acres of new surface water generate an abundance of hydroelectric power, contribute to flood control and irrigation, and greatly increase municipal water supplies. The largest and most expensive of the region's water projects to date has been the 446-mile long McLellan-Kerr Arkansas River Navigation System, linking the Tulsa Port of Catoosa with the Gulf Coast via the Arkansas and Mississippi Rivers. Built at a cost of $1.2 billion, the system has opened the way for improved shipping, and seven upstream reservoirs provide flood control, in addition to increasing the region's hydroelectric power.

Known early on as ''Tulsey Town'' (from the Creek word *tallasi*, meaning ''town''), the city of Tulsa, besides serving as the port of goods shipped into Oklahoma from the Gulf states, is better known as the self-proclaimed ''Oil Capital of the World.'' With more than 850 oil and oil-related companies based amid the city's shining high-rises, petroleum dominates Tulsa's economy. A giant statue of an oilman (The Golden Driller), his right arm resting on a derrick in front of Tulsa's Exposition Center, symbolizes the city's growth as an oil empire. Every three years the center plays host to the International Petroleum Exposition (the largest industrial trade show in the world), where visitors are awed by the Golden Driller's 55-foot height.

One of the more spectacular examples of the city's architecture is the Prayer Tower on the grounds of Oral Roberts University. A masterpiece of modern design, the 200-foot structure illuminates its surroundings at night with the glow from a lighted observation deck, which has a flame-tipped spire rising above it. The university's 500-acre campus, built at a cost of $55 million (and opened in 1965), is one of Tulsa's biggest tourist attractions. It stands as a monument to the one-time country boy from Pontococ County who first entered the city with $25 in his pocket, telling all who would listen, ''Expect a miracle.''

For the visitor interested in examining one of the finest collections of materials relating to the settling of the west, Tulsa's Thomas Gilcrease Institute of American History houses more than 200,000 primitive artifacts. Here are 60,000 rare books and manuscripts, together with 5,000 paintings and sculpture by such artists as Frederic Remington, Charles Russell, Thomas Moran, and Willard Stone. Complementing the exhibits of the Gilcrease Institute, but also bridging international boundaries, are the collections of the Philbrook Art Center. Formally the home of Waite Phillips (an Oklahoma pioneer), the Center now houses permanent displays of American Indian artifacts, paintings and sculpture of the Italian Renaissance, and unique examples of Chinese and African arts.

From Tulsa, one can drive southeast on the Muskogee Turnpike and within an hour arrive at the city for which the turnpike is named. Muskogee, like Tulsa, is strategically located on the Arkansas River Waterway, and is important as a manufacturing, wholesale, and distributing point. A city of 45,000, Muskogee prides itself on the wealth of its Indian heritage, many artifacts of which are on display at the Five Civilized Tribes Museum. Stressing the importance of preserving the region's ancient Indian arts, Bacone Indian College offers classes in art appreciation, as well as an academic program that draws many of its students from the surrounding Indian tribes. Also on the picturesque grounds of the college, the Ataloa Museum contains an outstanding collection of Indian art and jewelry, and thousands of books and documents on Indian history—a scholar's cornucopia.

Considered the city's most *colorful* tourist attraction, the azalea gardens of Muskogee's Honor Heights Park reach their picturesque peak about mid-April. Thousands are drawn here during Azalea Festival Days, when the park's 35,000 azaleas, comprising some 625 varieties, carpet the grounds with an array of bright colors. Begun as a park department promotion in 1967, the festival's attendance has risen from 50,000 visitors the first year, to a recent figure of more than 740,000. Visitors arrive by the busload, representing tourists from all over the United States. Included in the opening day festivities is the Azalea Parade (one of the southwest's largest), the Annual Miss Muskogee Pageant, and the newly-organized Azalea Auto Rallye.

Oklahoma City (the state's capital) and its surrounding communities of El Reno, Edmond, Norman, and Midwest City, dominate the geographical center of the state. Settled in the rush for the Unassigned Lands on April 22, 1889, this one-time "dusty depot on the sun-scorched prairie" acquired a population of nearly 10,000 between noon and sunset of the same day. A major cattle town in early years,

Oklahoma City gained its real economic strength after the rich oil strike in 1928. Oil derricks mushroomed over most of the eastern half of the city, even lining the State Capitol grounds to the very doorstep of the Capitol Building. Wells were drilled to unprecedented depths (at the time), some reaching 7,000 feet into the rich pool of black gold. Production sometimes exceeded 60,000 barrels a day from a single well, so enormous were the gas pressures seeking release from ages of entrapment. One well, the Mary Sudik, blew in with such force that it got out of control. At the rate of 35,000 barrels a day it spewed a column of oil to such a great height that the town of Norman, 15 miles to the south, received droplets from its spray.

To an outsider, Oklahoma City's ''forest of derricks'' seems an unfinished project, constructed of some giant erector set, out of context against the gleaming modern high-rises that have changed the face of Tulsa. Yet the city's residents seem comfortable with them, even to the point of displaying pictures of the wells that line the length of their Capitol grounds. The derrick of one of these wells stands where a petunia bed once bloomed, 431 feet from the center of the Capitol building. Completed in 1942, this well, and the others on the grounds, have contributed more than $8 million in revenue.

In addition to petroleum, Oklahoma City is also a leader in aircraft, livestock, and agricultural production. Some 750,000 people live in the city's metropolitan area, amid towering building complexes, plazas, malls, and fountains. Surrounded by choice recreational areas, the city's residents need only travel a short distance to immerse themselves in lush stands of timber, clear blue lakes, and a vast, open countryside. One can experience some of the flavor of the city's frontier days with a trip to the National Cowboy Hall of Fame and Western Heritage Center, where one will find a collection of paintings by Charles Russell, and exquisitely crafted bronze work by Frederic Remington. Perhaps the most moving of the exhibits is the 18-foot-high plaster statue by artist James Earle Fraser, titled ''End of the Trail.'' Portraying an Indian warrior, his spear cradled under his right arm with the tip pointing toward the ground, his finely sculptured body slumped astride a weary pony, the statue symbolizes the bitter defeat of a once proud people.

Spring and summer in Oklahoma City are the times for enjoying the beauty of the Annual Festival of Arts, basking on the shore of a scenic lake, visiting Lincoln Park Zoo, or listening to the music of local entertainers at beautiful Kerr Park in the city's downtown section. Visitors will find accommodations plentiful, with more than 8,000 rooms available at the city's inns. For large groups, the new Myriad Convention Center is one of the finest facilities of its kind in the United States.

Exuding (as Oklahoma's Chamber of Commerce brochures claim) a "special brand of western hospitality," the OK City is an exciting combination of yesterday, today, and tomorrow.

To the north of Oklahoma City, the town of Stillwater sports the beautiful campus of Oklahoma State University. Stillwater's OSU campus is the gathering place for livestock shows, food festivals, and organizations such as the Future Farmers of America and 4-H. Though considered to be the agricultural capital of the state, the town in recent years has created additional revenues with companies that produce rubber and paper products.

Agriculture also played an important part in the early growth of Ponca City, located north of Stillwater and close to the Kansas border. But from 1920 to 1930, oil filled the city's coffers with rich returns and doubled the town's population—prompting the popular saying that, Ponca was "built on oil, soil, and toil." One of Oklahoma's more famous statues is the 17-foot, six-ton monument of the "Pioneer Woman," located in a park adjacent to the town. Created by Bryan Baker (the result of an international competition financed by oil-baron E.W. Marland), the massive bronze captures the robust, determined features of a sunbonneted woman walking in hand with her son.

Fifteen miles to the east of Ponca City on State Highway 119 is beautiful Lake Kaw. Another of Oklahoma's projects for increasing water resources, Kaw boasts 17,000 acres of water and 169 miles of shoreline. Within a setting of low rolling hills and spacious grasslands, the lake has become a favorite of boaters and fishermen. Several varieties of bass, as well as catfish and crappie, will soon be augmented by deer and duck when a 16,254-acre public hunting area is fully developed. An additional 29,000 acres of water is contained by the 75-mile shoreline of Oologah Lake, about a half hour's drive from the outskirts of Tulsa. Translated from the Cherokee language, *Oologah* means "Dark Cloud," the lake and the town nearby being named in honor of the noted chief. Near the southern tip of the lake's western shore spreads the 993-acre Will Rogers State Park. Part of the old Clem Rogers Ranch, it was the birthplace of this famous American humorist.

Steeped in Indian heritage, colored with the beauties of woods and lakes amid vast open spaces, Northeastern Oklahoma is an exciting chapter from the state's past and present . . . one a visitor will not want to miss.

Wichita Mountains

Salyer Lake near Binger

Illinois River near Goats Bluff

Grande Lake O' The Cherokees

Farmhouse at sunset

Black Mesa State Park
(Following pages) Sunset Pool area, Wichita Mountains

Grand Lake O' The Cherokees

Red Rock Canyon State Park

27

Cascades above Turner Falls

Foss Reservoir

Illinois River near Flint Creek

Creek in Ouachita National Forest

Mount Scott area, Wichita Mountains

Glass Mountains
(Following pages) Wichita Mountains

Red Rock Park

Skyline Drive

Cucumber Creek Falls

Osage Lake, Wichita Mountains

Flowering field near Seiling

Lake Altus

Salyer Lake

Arbuckle Lake, Chickasaw National Recreation Area

Quartz Mountains

Red Rock Canyon State Park

Grasses in lake near Clinton

Quanah Park Lake, Wichita Wildlife Refuge

Bison at Wichita Mountains Wildlife Refuge

Peaceful lake scene

Late day sun on Oklahoma waters

54

A view from Winding Stair Mountains
(Following pages) Kulli Lake National Forest

Quachita National Forest

Washita River

Mount Scott, Wichita Mountains

Arbuckle Lake, Chickasaw National Recreation Area

Wichita Mountains

The Panhandle Region

The topography, as well as the climatic conditions of the eastern and western portions of Oklahoma, differ greatly. The Panhandle and most of the counties of the northwest section of the state lie within the High Plains region, much of it level grassland with low annual rainfall. There is a gentle tilt to the land, its highest point being Black Mesa at an elevation of nearly 5,000 feet, sloping to a low of 325 feet at the state's furthest southeastern point. Much of the northwest was marginal farmland, interspersed with ranches. During the drought years of the 1930s, this country underwent dust storms that ravaged its meager coating of top soil. Paul Schuster Taylor, writing of the dust bowl years in the book *An American Exodus*, said of it:

> "Dried by years of drought and pulverized by machine-drawn gang disk plows, the soil was literally thrown to the winds which whipped it in clouds across the country. The winds churned the soil, leaving vast stretches of farms blown and hummocked like deserts or the margins of beaches. They loosened the hold of settlers on the land, and like particles of dust drove them rolling down ribbons of highway.''

Today, deep-well irrigation, together with improved techniques in farming, have resurrected the land, enabling it to become a rich producer of wheat and feedgrain. Livestock, fattened by the region's plentiful harvests, supply a growing meat-packing industry. Oil also, as in other sections of the state, has contributed greatly to the region's recovery, heading the list of the area's largest employers.

Within the three counties that compose the actual panhandle of the state (Cimarron, Texas, and Beaver), Guymon, with a population of nearly 8,000, is the principal city. With the arrival of the Rock Island Railroad's main line in 1901, the growth of the town was assured; today it is considered the capital of the Panhandle. Two of the area's leading employers are Phillips Petroleum Company, and the meat-packing plant of Swift and Company. Record amounts of meats are processed from the livestock grown plump at the troughs of highly automated feed lots. Starting the first weekend in May, thousands of visitors are attracted to Guymon to share in the festivities of the Pioneer Days Celebration. It is a rollicking funfest that offers huge chuck-wagon feeds and an exciting carnival atmosphere. Close by, the town of Goodwell is worth a visitor's side trip for the historical exhibits in its No Man's Land Museum. Many of the exhibits reflect the history of Oklahoma's unclaimed sections.

Nearly centrally located in Beaver County to the east of Guymon is the small town of Beaver City. During mid-April the town holds the annual Cimarron Territory Celebration and features an event not likely to be seen in Olympic competition—the world championship Cow Chip Throwing Contest. The contest recalls the days when dried buffalo droppings were gathered for fuel for heating and cooking. The object of the contest is to throw your chip the farthest. The record stands at 152 feet.

Moving east out of the Panhandle into the counties of Harper, Woodward, and Ellis, one enters a major park and recreational area. Just southwest of the town of Freedom, off State Highway 50, is Alabaster Caverns State Park. Here tunnels of pink, white, and vari-colored alabaster, highlighted by the sparkle of selenite crystals, awe the visitor. They are the world's largest alabaster cave formations. A short drive southwest of the caverns will bring one to Boiling Springs State Park and into a heavily timbered area with a four-acre lake. Numerous cold springs bubbling up through the park's white sands contribute to the boiling effect, which gives the park its name.

As one crosses the Canadian River just west of Boiling Springs, the town of Woodward (trade center for a wide farming and ranching area) offers additional recreational space within a 15-acre city park, Crystal Beach. Golfing, swimming, and tennis are the favorite sports here. The Pioneer Museum and Art Center on the south end of the town contains a fine collection of Indian artifacts, western art, and early 1900 fashions. For those visiting the town in July, the Woodard Elks Rodeo—four days of hooting and hollering—draws the best riders and ropers in the nation to display their rugged skills. The population of the city has nearly doubled in 20 years, the result of a healthy industrial growth bolstered by the presence of some 100 petroleum-related companies.

Northwest of the town of Cheyenne, in Roger Mills County, is the site of the infamous Washita Massacre. Here 500 troops from the 7th cavalry, led by Colonel George Armstrong Custer, surprised a village of peaceful southern Cheyenne. During the ensuing battle, the Cheyenne chief, Black Nettle, together with his wife and some 100 men, women and children lost their lives. Custer had attacked while the Indians slept and the defeat was nearly total, with the exception of a few warriors that had managed to escape, pursued by a squad of troopers. Custer and his remaining troops captured 53 women and children. Before returning to their camp, they burned the entire village and slaughtered 875 horses.

South of the area of the Washita Massacre, U.S. Highway 283 connects with Interstate 40, where its northeastern route will take the visitor past the cities of Elk, Clinton, and Weatherford. Elk's Old Town Museum features turn-of-the-century gingerbread-style architecture, its decor allowing one a look at authentic Victorian furnishings. For exhibits relating to the region's pioneer and Indian life, Clinton's Western Trails Museum will trigger imaginings of Oklahoma's colorful past. Weatherford is largely a college town; nearly two-thirds of its population is enrolled in Southern State University. The principal recreational area for this three-city region lies just northwest of Clinton, the popular 8,800-acre Lake Foss. It is the home of Washita National Wildlife Refuge, offering plentiful camping and picnic facilities.

Enid is northwestern Oklahoma's largest city, one whose diversified economy includes a large agri-business community and one of the world's biggest producers of oil and water drilling equipment. Settled almost instantly during the Cherokee Outlet land rush of 1863, the town could even boast of an instant railroad, since the Rock Island Railroad had already laid tracks through the area. The surrounding Garfield County area literally grows its own gold, in the form of wheat fields, which carpet huge sections of the countryside. With a storage capacity of over 66-million bushels, Enid leads the state in storing, processing, and marketing of grain. Also adding to the town's economy, Vance Air Force Base, south of Enid, pays out more than $8 million annually to some 2,000 military and civilian employees.

In his book *The Cherokee Strip*, Marquis James has written an engaging account of his early childhood in Enid. His recollections detail the excitement of a young boy exploring the countryside, not many years after the first rush of homesteaders had staked their claims. Lying in a patch of grass on the rim of a bluff overlooking Boggy Creek, the boy and his dog surveyed the scene below:

> "The rim was about my favorite place on the whole claim . . . below lay the dark, plowed earth of West Bottom, which we sometimes called the Horseshoe from the way Boggy Creek curved around it. Lazying in from the Schrock claim on the other side of the Bottom, old Boggy's winding course was defined by a string of elms and cottonwoods whose branches the opening buds bathed in a pale green haze."

And of a trip to the town itself:

> "A trip to Enid was surely a marvelous treat, the stairways one saw being
> the very least of it. First off, on the edge of the prairie was a house here and a
> house there—and not so many of them sod houses, either. Quite a few were
> even painted . . . . [One] house was painted yellow, like ours. It had an upstairs.
> As I could see no ladder (and I looked sharply) there must have been a stair-
> case *inside*."

West of Enid, between Cleo Springs and Aline, one can view an original
"soddy," the type still common when James was a boy. Cut from the tough prairie
in manageable blocks, the dark sod was piled brick-like until it formed the dwelling's
four walls. Sticks were then laid as roof beams and overlaid with lighter chunks of
earth to complete the shelter. Though moisture was a constant problem—seepage
kept the walls damp at all times—the sod houses were perfect insulators, staying cool
during the hottest of summers, and warm in the most bitter of winters.

Held in by a 68-foot high dam constructed in 1941 by the Corp of Engineers,
the waters of the 9,300-acre Great Salt Plains Reservoir lie just northeast of Enid.
Besides the excellent fishing in the area, a National Wildlife Refuge is a popular
gathering place for nature lovers throughout the state. Nature trails are numerous,
allowing visitors a chance to view some of the area's abundant animal life: deer, quail,
wild turkey, and many species of birds. Another favorite pastime is digging for
selenite crystals on the wide salt flats at the lake's mouth—believed by some to be the
remains of an ancient salt sea.

Southeast of Enid, and a short distance north of Oklahoma City, lies the one-time
capital of Oklahoma, Guthrie. Already having a post office two weeks before the
territory was officially opened for settlement, the town gained 15,000 persons by
nightfall of the first day of the run. The year 1910 saw the town's capital status
stolen by Oklahoma City, after a statewide vote. Still standing is the Cooperative
Publishing Company building, home of Oklahoma's first newspaper, located in
Guthrie's downtown section. Within the same area are many of the city's historic
homes, some of which are being fully restored with National Park Service assistance
since the area has been declared an Historic District.

Northwestern Oklahoma is a blending of many fascinating topographical
features that extend from the semi-arid Panhandle counties, to the region's greener,
more centralized parklands. The historical drama of the land's early settlement still
lingers, its ambience strengthened by many historical waysides and displays of
important artifacts. Here a visitor is offered, in all its colorful variety, a view of the
early west.

Southwest

The transition between Texas and Oklahoma would go unnoticed by a traveler if it were not for the sinuous path of the Red River marking the boundary. Great vistas of short grass are common to the region, their tenacious hold on the land supporting limited grazing. Irrigation and crop rotation have rescued much of what had become unproductive farmland, due to shortsighted farming methods. Yet farmers of the region still keep a wary eye toward the skies, knowing that endless days of strong winds and sunny weather might signal a dry spell even modern farming methods and deep well irrigation could fail to handle.

As one moves toward the city of Lawton, near southwestern Oklahoma's interior, the rough granite tops of the Wichita Mountains can be seen, sharply contrasting against the surrounding plains. Lawton, Comanche county seat and third largest of Oklahoma's cities, is another of the state's overnight settlements. On August 6, 1901, homesteaders poured into the new city after two million acres of Kiowa-Comanche-Apache Reservation land was opened to white settlement. Today the town's industry is subordinate to the moneys that flow from the adjoining Fort Still Military Reservation, prime contributor to Lawton's growth as a city. The fort's 95,000 acres spread into the rugged Wichita Mountains, and visitors are welcome to explore the grounds on a daily basis. Many of the fort's original stone buildings are still in use, their appearance adding to the frontier atmosphere. Most famous of these is the guardhouse where Chief Geronimo was held captive, spending many of his years confined in a basement cell.

For visitors to the area, the main recreational attraction lies within the heavily eroded contours of the Wichita Mountains and its adjacent wildlife refuge. Much of the area is blanketed by low scrub, but in parts of its northwestern section, trees and clear streams highlight the 59,000 acre refuge. Since 1907 (two years after the land was proclaimed a game preserve), buffalo have prospered within the protective boundaries, their numbers increasing to hundreds from a small herd of 15, introduced to guard against their threatened extinction. Prospering here are herds of

69

elk and antelope, and large numbers of white-tailed deer. A paved road leading to the summit of Mount Scott (at 2,467 feet), numerous lakes, and ten camp and picnic areas are among the attractions that draw a million or more visitors here annually.

As one travels east of Lawton, the land takes on a greener aspect. Large herds of cattle roam vast, well-tended ranchlands. Though the scars of previous wasteful farming methods are still in evidence, they are fast being covered. One soon encounters the town of Duncan, settled in 1892, and now home for a population of some 20,000. Thousands of longhorns were once herded past the spot the town now occupies, during dusty drives from Texas to railheads in Kansas on the old Chisholm Trail. The town's economy depended heavily on agriculture until an oil-well cementing service moved here in 1921 (Halliburton Services). Through spectacular growth (its products are now sent world wide), Halliburton employs more than ten percent of the citizenry.

North of Duncan, edging the H.E. Bailey Turnpike, the city of Chickasha bills herself as ''The Queen City of the Washita Valley.'' The rich soil of the valley is responsible for her agricultural excellence, but oil in recent years has grown in importance, with a number of 1,000-barrel-a-day wells pumping new wealth into her economy. The nearby campus of the University of Science and Arts of Oklahoma is this area's cultural center. In addition to an annual art show on the grounds, there are also concerts, plays, and informative lectures. Principal recreation centers upon Lake Chickasha, a 1,900-acre municipal reservoir located 15 miles northwest of the town—offering hunting, fishing, and watersports.

The town of Anadarko is rich in the history of the Southern Plains Indian. Located just west of Chickasha, the town is considered the Plains Indian capital of the state. Numerous exhibits capture the city's Indian heritage with displays of cultural and historical interest. Beautifully crafted Indian wares can be purchased at the town's Southern Plains Indian Museum and Crafts Center. Opposite it, the American Indian Hall of Fame is a showcase for exquisitely cast bronze busts of great Indian leaders, combined with exhibits pertaining to their lives. Anadarko is the headquarters for the bureaus and agencies that see to the welfare of some 26,000 Indians in western Oklahoma and Kansas.

The area's most impressive visitors attraction is located just six miles south of Anadarko—Indian City, U.S.A. Here, a 45-minute guided tour will take one through seven authentically reconstructed Indian villages (Caddo, Kiowa, Apache, Pueblo, Navajo, Pawnee, and Wichita). A craft shop on the complex offers the visitor unique examples of pottery, jewelry, and beadwork, and in the summer months colorful Indian dances provide the entertainment.

A short drive northwest of Anadarko lie the sport and recreation facilities of Fort Cobb Reservoir. In addition to the watersports provided at the lake, 3,500 adjoining acres have been set aside by the state as a public hunting area, and 4,500 for a state park. Although the park is a refuge for the wildlife of the area, hunters flock to other nearby sections to participate in one of Oklahoma's major sports—crow hunting. It seems the big black birds have developed a fondness for the menu offered by the local peanut and feed-grain growers, and have chosen to spend their winter months in the area—a gathering that sometimes totals six million of the belligerent birds.

Altus is southwestern Oklahoma's second largest city. Located at the junction of U.S. Highway 283 and 62, about 45 miles west of Lawton, the city has counted heavily on agriculture and the government moneys that flow through the Military Airlift Command at the city's edge for its continued growth. Settlers in the area were driven to the town's present site after a flood on Bitter Creek destroyed many of their homes in 1891. Many artifacts relating to the area's history are contained in the town's Museum of the Western Prairie, its unique construction duplicating the design of a half-dugout—a design very similar to the first dwellings of the region's pioneer settlers.

Altus Reservoir, north of Altus, is a 6,770-acre oasis in the rugged Quartz Mountain area. Portions of the lake's 49 miles of shoreline include complete camping facilities, where fishing, picnicking, swimming, and waterskiing are favorite pastimes. A public hunting area at the lake's north end is another popular location for crow shooters. Large numbers of the birds take up winter residence there.

Semi-arid and given to fits of wind-blown anger, southwestern Oklahoma presents a unique face to the visitor. One will see its harsher aspects lined in the faces of farmers and written on the land's surface, where erosion has worn deep red gullies. One will also see where reclamation efforts have gradually created choice recreational areas and salvaged vast tracks of farmland from the dry landscape. Most important, a visitor here will be able to view remnants of a once-great culture.

Beautiful America Publishing Company

The nation's foremost publisher of quality color photography

Current Books

Alaska, Arizona, British Columbia, California, California Vol. II, California Coast, California Desert, California Missions, Colorado, Florida, Georgia, Hawaii, Idaho, Las Vegas, Los Angeles, Michigan, Michigan Vol. II, Minnesota, Montana, Montana Vol. II, Mt. Hood (Oregon), New York, New Mexico, Northern California, Northern California Vol. II, North Carolina, North Idaho, Ohio, Oklahoma, Oregon, Oregon Vol. II, Oregon Coast, Oregon Country, Pennsylvania, Pittsburgh, San Diego, San Francisco, San Juan Islands, Seattle, Texas, Utah, Vancouver U.S.A., Virginia, Washington, Washington Vol. II, Washington D.C., Wisconsin, Wyoming, Yosemite National Park

Forthcoming Books

Beauty of Oregon, Beauty of Washington, California Mountains, Chicago, Dallas, Denver, Illinois, Indiana, Kentucky, Maryland, Massachusetts, Mississippi, Missouri, Nevada, New Jersey, New York City, Ozarks, Pacific Coast, Rocky Mountains, South Carolina, Tennessee, Vermont

Large Format, Hardbound Books

Beautiful America, Beauty of California, Glory of Nature's Form, Lewis & Clark Country, Western Impressions